Private Label Selling For Beginners:

Find Manufacturers, Build Your Brand and Sell Products as Your Own Using Amazon FBA, eBay and Other Business Models

By

Dale Blake

Table of Contents

Introduction 5

Chapter 1. Starting Your Private Label Business 6

Chapter 2. Identifying Your Market 10

Chapter 3. Choosing Private Label Products 13

Chapter 4. Where to Source Your Private Label Product ... 16

Chapter 5. Selling Your Private Label Products 19

Chapter 6. Understanding Your Profit Margins 21

Chapter 7. Marketing Strategies 25

Chapter 8. Pros and Cons of Private Labeling 29

Conclusion 32

Thank You Page 33

Private Label Selling For Beginners: Find Manufacturers, Build Your Brand and Sell Products as Your Own Using Amazon FBA, eBay and Other Business Models

By Dale Blake

© Copyright 2015 Dale Blake

Reproduction or translation of any part of this work beyond that permitted by section 107 or 108 of the 1976 United States Copyright Act without permission of the copyright owner is unlawful. Requests for permission or further information should be addressed to the author.

This publication is designed to provide accurate and authoritative information in regard to the subject matter covered. This work is sold with the understanding that the publisher is not engaged in rendering legal, accounting, or other professional services. If legal advice or other expert assistance is required, the services of a competent professional person should be sought.

First Published, 2015

Printed in the United States of America

Introduction

In business, reputation matters. Very few merchants and consumers will readily buy from an unknown company. While these nests in sensible grounds that experience will always beget top quality products, manufacturers entering the market with innovative products will always be at a disadvantage unless they throw lot with the professionals. This happens in the most symbiotic relationships in our modern day markets known as private label selling.

With private label selling, the inventor or manufacturer will contact an established brand seller and have him or her distribute products under their name. In this way, the brand name makes a profit and the inventor get more and more of their product to the market. An alternative approach to the matter is private label sellers approaching manufacturers with the proposition. Starting this business and convincing the manufacturer that you are the right brand to get those better sells is a delicate task that needs elaborate preparations.

Chapter 1. Starting Your Private Label Business

Before venturing into the market, you first have to set up a fully functional private label company. This means that you have to handle all the local legalities pertaining to registration and certification of the business before you can begin selling. Failure to do this could pit you against the local authorities. Alternatively, this could reduce how seriously the companies you contact will take you. Other than just registering, you will need a couple of other tricks up your sleeve to set things in motion.

Constant evaluation of customers and consumers purchasing habits means that they are always looking for better ways to get the best value for their dollars. This explains the recent upswing of private label companies and businesses stores with strong brand name quality tend to have a grip on the customers as they attract more people. Here are some of the things you can follow to build a great private label company for yourself.

Find the appropriate products

Do not join the list of many retailers whose mistake is to take too long to decide on the product or commodity to deal with. It is important to establish a line of product that you want to specialize in and slowly start introducing clients to it. This will also help you to launch products that will target a specific customer group.

Understand what products meet the needs of your target audience before investing in it. You need to strive on getting a customer to take as many products as they can from your stores, as this is a means of making yourself stay relevant to them. However, exercise caution not to buy too many products that will take you down especially if customers are not interested in them.

Brand yourself

Creating a private labeling line goes beyond offering customers an alternative. It involves presenting a completely new brand, which customers can open their eyes to and benefit from. It should include giving low price offers. Your brand should be identified by its appearance thus the need to be keen with the design process.

Do not go for too complex logos as they are only more confusing and show lack of professionalism. Get a professional artist or designer to balance the colors as this is very crucial when dealing with private labeling. The labeling should not hinder you from making any necessary changes whenever they arise.

Be creative

When a retailer is not innovative enough this could lead to his or her downfall. Launching a product with no national brand is risky but can lead to great success. Choose a manufacturer that is innovative enough to create products that are unique and exceptional. The manufacturer should be able to bring to the table something that is credible and stands out.

The fact that retailers have a unique knowledge of customers need and wants should be a motivation for buying exactly what customers are asking for. Innovations in different things such as ingredients, delivery systems and packaging are what contribute to the growth of private label business.

Extra credit

Let the fact that you are stocking a product that another company also private label's it not deter you from pursuing your own goals. You never know what brand a customer is likely to pick. You should strive to create a brand so unique and different that customers will want to be associated with. In addition to this make sure that you choose decide before bringing in products if the new product is going to bring you sales or take away the existing ones.

Chapter 2. Identifying Your Market

Private label markets today are carefully managed and marketed in order to improve retailer's competitive edge. In fact, they are seen as well established brands. This is the reason why identifying your market is a crucial step to gaining success in this industry.

Consider the target audience/ customer group

Observe the national and local trends that your product takes. You can look at what competitors are doing that attracts customers. Based on this, you will be able to manipulate your customers' interest. If most customers prefer products that do not scream private label then you should invest in artisanal words and imagery that appeal to the customers.

Choose the right strategy either for the market the up or down strategy

Despite the rapid market, growth there still exists some untapped opportunities. It is important to use a strategy that will guarantee consistent and desirable branding of your product. Based on the audience you are targeting, this is likely to happen or fail to be. A good example would be when the product you sell banks on seasonal interest such as football meaning that you are not assured of continuous markets unlike baby products whose market will never lack as babies are born every day. The product you sell also influences the market.

Consumer purchase habits

Find out how frequent customers buy certain products and what influences their decisions. In case you notice an upward trend for labeled products then you should focus on tapping into this market. Chances are that consumers trust labeled products more because of the excellent branding.

The market identification phase will help you settle for a product that will sell. This is the most crucial aspect of the search. Go for things that are useful in your target market but are unavailable, in low supply or whatever the market has on offer are expensive and of inferior quality.

The last check to take your product of choice through before making the decision is how wieldy it is. There is no way to emphasize how important it is to get something that you can move around easily and conveniently. The ease of transporting your products will depend on the initial investment into the business. If you are willing to put into place elaborate plans, then you can go for bulky but dear products that have to be imported. You however have to go through all the import logistics and determine the final cost of each unit before deeming it worth the effort.

Chapter 3. Choosing Private Label Products

The following are some of the things you must look at when choosing a private label product.

Profitable market and high demand

The product you are selling must be profitable based on its demand rate. The idea may be amazing but this is to enough. The product may be appealing to you but may not translate to a product that people will demand for. You can find out from certain selling sites such as Amazon to find out the highly ranking products. This proof of concept when entering the market will give you the necessary confidence that you too can succeed with your products.

Reasonable competition

You may get a market that demands your products highly and attracts a high potential but the competition deters you from choosing the product. When the market is too competitive, you may have a hard time competing with the top ranking products. Some of competition has been selling specific products for years giving them a wealth of experience, money and knowledge to get themselves ranked at the top.

The product should sell more than a specific price

You should be sure that the product you choose could sell more than a specific price say 10 dollars o Amazon and other sites. This is the only way to avoid getting the product being categorized as an add-on item but instead raked as a main product. After all, you want your product to be bought directly and not through another.

Easy to stock

Unless you are dealing with perishables like flowers and vegetables, you should always go for products with longer shelf lives. You do not want your entire consignment going bad before you can sell it. Moreover, you should also consider the structure of the products and pay attention to wieldy and hardy goods.

Again, easy to stock is relative. It depends on the infrastructure you have in place and the much you are willing to spend. Matching your product with your capabilities is key to establishing a balanced out label selling business.

Chapter 4. Where to Source Your Private Label Product

Alibaba

Alibaba is China's largest online commerce company. It perhaps one of the biggest in the world. With Alibaba, you get into contact with the true manufacturer and sort out the deal by interacting directly with the manufacturer. Since it is the busiest e-commerce platform, you can be sure of getting reputable deals from some of the most affordable and well-established dealers in the market.

Aliexpress

Aliexpress is another platform that links merchants with manufacturers from China and other Asian region countries. The good thing about sourcing products from these manufacturers is that the total cost of laying your hands onto a product, with the shipping costs inclusive, is always lower than that of purchasing locally or manufacturing them on your own. You should however ensure that you are dealing with a highly rated manufacturer to ensure that you get top quality products off the deal.

Global Sources

Global Sources is a Hong Kong business to business company whose main goal is to facilitate trade between businesses. This makes it a perfect deal since it has all the logistics of joining you to the manufacturer in place. All you have to do is identify the seller, do the reviews and place an order. Since it will provide you with information about the supplier, you can easily rate a seller's credibility and make trade-offs between a couple of deals before making the final purchase. The e-commerce site authenticates each manufacturer before putting them into its directory.

Manufucturers.com

As the name suggests, this is a place dedicated to manufacturers. With this site, you will be in contact with the actual manufacturers regardless of their native location. This means that if you believe better quality products comes from a specific geographical location, you always are at liberty of making the purchase at that specific country. This will however present you with the price and profit margin analysis, something you should do thoroughly if you are to identify the perfect deal for your private label selling business.

Google search

The final approach and perhaps most versatile one is doing a simple Google search with the appropriate keywords. You will get a list of online merchants who can sell you the products in bulk. Some of them could be individual business while others could be e-commerce platforms like the ones mentioned above.

Chapter 5. Selling Your Private Label Products

You could decide to sell your products in person using a physical shop or sell them online. Selling online could be more lucrative since a huge number of people are doing their shopping online. In this case, you again have to choose between online selling platforms and using your own e-shop.

Online selling platforms

Online selling platforms include already existent seller sites like eBay, Amazon FBA and Shopify. With such websites, all you have to do is create a profile and list your goods as a merchant. The process is fairly simple and there are no many limitations on who can or cannot sell. Even though these sites will slash off a percentage of your profits, you must understand that they will help you reach out to more and more customers especially when on your maiden run.

Amazon and eBay are already established selling platforms. They have thousands of visitors per minutes meaning that the chances of exposing your product in this platform are higher. Using simple tricks like fair pricing, perfect description and use of good images could give you the competitive edge over your rivals.

Your own e-shop

Setting up your own e-commerce website should be, and must be your ultimate goal. With an e-commerce website under your private label, you stand a better chance at establishing yourself as a brand and drawing more and more customers to you. You might need a professional web designer to help you create, implement and manage the online shop.

Chapter 6. Understanding Your Profit Margins

Due to the changes in economies with recession hitting most markets, many consumers have been seen rushing towards private label goods. The word wide demand for these products has been seen to increase tremendously probably because of their fair pricing. Economic downturn has seen most people buying store brands. This has seen a steady rise in profits for industry players.

Private portfolio

Private label brands are commanding a profit margin of between 60-90 percent for retailers. This explains the rising push towards more store-only brands. The rate label industry will continue to grow due to this push and the dragging economic status.

Costs and profit margins

Retailers strive to provide the best for the target clientele. A successful management team understands that the failure or success of a company is built from ground up. In an otherwise perfect world, retailers would offer their clients the highest product quality and entice them with the lowest prices. However, this is not practical in the real world especially considering the element of profit taking.

Usually brand names come with a higher price tag. There could be a 20% increase just due to the brand name. This is not because the brand name can get away with higher expenses but also due to the shipping costs of the product from the warehouse to the distributors and individual businesses all of which want to make profit. All these factors coming into play will explain why a product will have an increase in price as well as the reason why retailers have little control over their own inventory.

The retailer may end up with an overstocked shelf or one, which is understocked due to these factors. At times there may be need to disposed outdated products that could have generated income thus causing, loses. This explains why private label products will be given an upper hand due to its fair pricing and higher profits.

With this out of the way, you can now start thinking of the real manufacturers to deal with. The simplest places to get these sellers could be on eBay, Amazon or Alibaba. These sites will help you get the most viable suppliers who have the power to deliver the right product whenever you need it. Choosing a supplier who can deliver the right product and let you change the labeling as you please is key to your success.

An alternative would be making your search on Google. Use a simple keyword relevant to the market you have chosen and add supplier at the end. This will give you the true suppliers of unbranded product, if not the manufacturers. In this way, you can lay your hands to the original product that will work best for you.

Remember that profit is dependent on both the cost of purchasing the products and the much you spend in converting the products into a brand. If you need $500 to purchase a stock and $100 to label to label it up, you will then need to sell the products at an individual cost that surpasses this amount.

Another thing that could let you miss out on the profit margin is assuming the transportation and sales costs. Since these go into the delivery of the product to the market, they should also contribute to its pricing hence the profit margin.

The idea here is to work with a product that gives you a comfortable profit margin without necessarily blowing things out of proportions. To achieve this, you could either chose to work with something you can brand and resell cheaply or go with rare products that do not have ready competition in your local market.

Chapter 7. Marketing Strategies

Private label marketing is the easiest way to get your products shelf space in most retail stores. This however does not qualify it for advertising campaigns support. This is why you need to get the strategy right for you to make something out of the whole venture. There are different ways through which you can form successful private- label buyers' relationships as discussed below.

Simplify things

Making things easier for buyers by requesting a purchase order is in order. This will help you supply the buyer's package as ordered or modify it to meet his or her specifications. It is also important to offer training to sales people and offer to maintain a website for the product. You may come with displays and diagrammatic representations of what complementary products should be displayed next.

Pay attention to products

A private-label buyer will is likely not to invest any money in marketing. This means that any potential buyers need to see and realize the importance of your product to them. Take time to package and brand your consumer product in order to sell it yourself. The packaging and design of the product are important if the agreement is with a retailer.

Offer top-notch service

This means that you need to provide marketing support including attending trade fairs and shows, publicity release, active web page work and offering brochures or ads layouts. You can also offer to handle the customer service task whereby you deal with complaints, product returns and relaying customers' improvement suggestions to the manufacturer.

Understand how to deal with your competition

Most companies take private –labels initiatives to stay ahead of their competition. In order to sell this concept effectively you need to know your competition and understand how the manufacturing company of your products can improve them in line with the competitors. The familiarity with competition also helps when it comes to retailing especially if it is meant to be your last stop.

You can always find potential private-label partners by conducting an internet search. You can also check manufacturers associations who host trade shows and have relevant information on the same. It is important to take several precautions before approaching any company.

Take care of your own business protection

Companies buying private-labels are not keen about patent status. Even so, you do not want to take the risk of a company owning the product or a competitor stealing your idea and introducing a similar product in the market.

Proto types

Look alike will definitely flood the market the moment you release your brand. For this reason, most companies will want to test and see how the product forms before they can settle for your brand.

Research before hand

You should never approach a manufacturer with a private-label proposal until you are sure that there is a ready market and demand for your products.

Companies want to see proof of existing target market. This you can do by providing survey reports or supporting letter from influential users.

While working as a private label seller might be great for business especially if you do not have the necessary infrastructure. This doesn't mean that this business will be a smooth breeze. No. There are a couple of things to take into consideration before starting your business. Understanding when to or not to venture into this business plan will help you mitigate any situations before they occur.

Chapter 8. Pros and Cons of Private Labeling

There are many things one needs to consider before deciding if it is a good idea to start a private label company. You need to weigh both pros and cons before making any conclusive decisions. The following are some of the things that must be looked into before taking this bold step.

Pros

Cost is one of the most important things that all business startups consider before going any farther. When you decide to venture into private labeling the startup costs comes down drastically and unlike a proprietary business where several thousand dollars are needed for a startup, private labeling involves using as little as hundred dollars to get started.

The other advantage is the fact that all services are included in private labeling. The product manufacturer in most cases is involved with product manufacturing only thus any other services such as labeling, packing and shipping will have to be outsourced. You may also have to take care of your own hazard control, which is not a cheap affair. When you choose to private label your company all these services will be included and it is especially helpful when it comes to dealing with the insurance part.

There are unique products in probate labeling than most people think of. While there cannot lack crappy companies that make the whole industry look bad, a few good companies exist. These companies have diverse products to offer. Furthermore it is often taken for garneted that almost all products are private labeled in some sort of way.

Most customers base their purchasing decisions on how products look on the shelves hence the need to opt for private labeling. It is especially more important for those people who have a knack for design and a nose for marketing as they are likely to know the difference better.

Cons

However, even with the many advantages of private labeling companies, it is important to look at the other side of things. You need to know how much of a disadvantage you are placing yourself into especially

Conclusion

Private label selling businesses are a great way to getting to the market without investing into your own manufacturing plant. In most cases, it lets you take advantage of the economies of scale as you will be buying goods in bulk and packaging them into smaller but expensive packages. In this way, you stand the chance of making a sound profit and establishing a product name of your own.

Since it is any other business, you also have to invest some time and money in building the right infrastructure to propel you into the market. This could include a social media presence and elaborate marketing strategies geared towards making your brand more popular. If you are doing it on your own, do your research well. There so many pitfalls and a thousand and one ways in which you can make your venture more profitable. Exploiting these is the only sure way to making a good profit off your venture.

because you are selling the exact same product that someone else is selling. This will vary depending on various things and the risk could be small or large.

It is not advisable to go into private label if your aim is to join retail market, target widespread distribution or looking for outside money. You will always be curtailed by many things top on the list being failure to lower your price enough, failure to be unique and outstanding as well as the fact that you will be dealing with a customer group of highly informed people.

Private labeling makes sense when you are dealing with people who sell locally such as professionals like doctors, gyms and grocery stores. Clients who are market testing are another great target group. You can effectively manage your marketing campaign with private labeling when you are working with a tight or squeezed budget. Those without budget options can also consider private labeling and those looking to fill the gaps in their products lines which tend to happen a lot.

Thank You Page

I want to personally thank you for reading my book. I hope you found information in this book useful and I would be very grateful if you could leave your honest review about this book. I certainly want to thank you in advance for doing this.

If you have the time, you can check my other books too.

CPSIA information can be obtained
at www.ICGtesting.com
Printed in the USA
LVHW04s1647120618
580463LV00012B/234/P